FIVE

5

FIVE

versus

THE REST OF THE WORLD

FIVE *versus* THE REST OF THE WORLD

JANE PRESTON

EBURY
PRESS

First published in Great Britain in 1999

10 9 8 7 6 5 4 3 2 1

Ebury Press
Random House
20 Vauxhall Bridge Road
London SW1 2SA

Random House Australia Pty Limited
20 Alfred Street, Milsons Point
Sydney
New South Wales 2061, Australia

Random House New Zealand Limited
18 Poland Road, Glenfield, Auckland 10
New Zealand

Random House South Africa (Pty) Limited
Endulini, 5A Jubilee Road
Parktown 2193
South Africa

Random House UK Limited Reg. No. 954009

A CIP catalogue record for this book is available from the British Library

ISBN 0-09-187177-8

Papers used by Ebury Press are natural, recyclable products made
from wood grown in sustainable forests

Polaroid photographs © Five
All others © Dave Willis for Idols Licensing and Publicity Ltd

Designed by Blackjacks

Printed in Great Britain at the University Press, Cambridge

Contents

Thanx for your Support, thanx for buying our Singles. This is our Second book, Hope you enjoy it.

Thanx
5ive

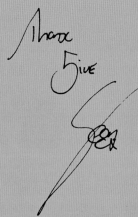

Ho!!.. This is me saying thank you and thanking you for your support.

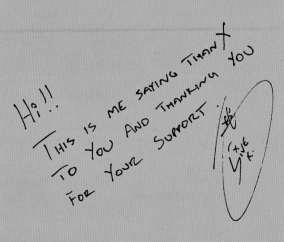

Thanx for buying the book and supporting five. if you're in the shop just reading it then Please Please buy it Thanx again

Lots ur Love

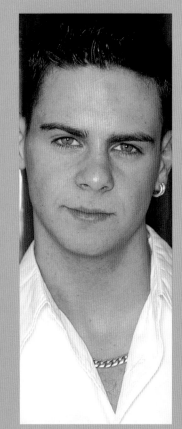

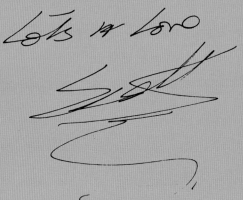

Yet another massive
THANK YOU to all the fans.
Heres the second book & hope you
like the second Album. thanks for all the support

Loads of Love

Ritchie
& Sue

Hello —
Thanx once again
for buying this book.
It's not a waste of money
cos' I'm in it !!!
Enjoy !!!

Introduction

TWO YEARS ago Five didn't exist – yet today they are one of the most successful male bands in the world! Scott, Ritchie, J, Abs and Sean's meteoric rise to international fame has been a combination of serious talent, hard work – and the vision of two men who had a dream...

Pop svengalis Bob and Chris Herbert, a father and son team who run the management company Safe, were the brains behind the scenes who created the Spice Girls. They knew the time was right to unleash a new kind of band on the pop world – so they decided to follow Girl Power with Lad Power!

They searched to find five blokes who were not only good-looking and talented, but also had the attitude to set them apart from other pop bands. It wasn't an easy task. Bob and Chris slogged through 3,000 hopefuls at open auditions held all over the country before deciding on the final line-up.

They had decided to make the band a four-bloke group, but when they saw Scott, Abs, Ritchie, J and Sean perform together they

WORLDWIDE SINGLES SALES

Slam Dunk (da Funk)	500,000
When The Lights Go Out	1,110,000
Got The Feeling	600,000
Everybody Get Up	700,000
Until The Time Is Through	450,000

knew there was no way they could split them apart. 'As soon as we saw the five guys together we just knew they had what it takes – both character-wise and musically' says Bob. 'It was obvious that they were perfect together. We had found our band.'

So Five were born! All they had to do now was get down to the serious job of making the band a force to be reckoned with. But before they could begin, the lads had to get to know, like and trust each other! Like the Spice Girls before them, the group moved into a house in Camberley, Surrey, to help them really click together as a unit. Living together 24/7 became a bonding exercise – a dress-rehearsal for what lay ahead.

Five quickly gelled as a band and – after touring the country on the Smash Hits Roadshow – were soon ready to stake their claim on the British charts. The debut single, 'Slam Dunk (da Funk)', crashed in at Number 10 – and the album *Five* went straight in at Number 1. Five followed it up with four scorching Top 10 singles.

With such awesome debut success, there was no question about it – Five were on their way to the top! The next step was to conquer the world. The lads have taken no prisoners as they've travelled the planet spreading the pop gospel according to Five. As Ritchie, Scott, J, Sean and Abs will tell you, they are a team of five lads united in the pursuit of one magnificent dream – to make Five the biggest band in the world!

The rest, as they say, will be history!

Five fans around the world

Living together 24/7 became a bonding exercise – a dress-rehearsal for what lay ahead.

WORLDWIDE ALBUM SALES

Nearly 4 million worldwide album sales.

PLATINUM DISCS:

Argentina
Australia x3
Belgium
Canada
Denmark
Indonesia x3
Ireland x5
Italy x2
Malaysia x2
New Zealand x4
Philippines
Sweden x2
Taiwan
Thailand
UK x2
USA

GOLD DISCS:

Chile
Holland
Israel
Korea
Singapore
Spain

scott hogs the MTV gong

MUSIC AWARDS

Rock Bear (Denmark)	Winners of Best International Newcomer
Popcorn (Greece)	Winners of Best International Band
Brits (UK)	Nominated for Best Newcomer Award
Smash Hits (UK)	Winners of Best UK Band, Best Album, Best Album Cover and Best Haircut (Scott)
MTV Europe	MTV Select Award
TMF (Holland)	Winners of Best Single, Best Album and Best International Group

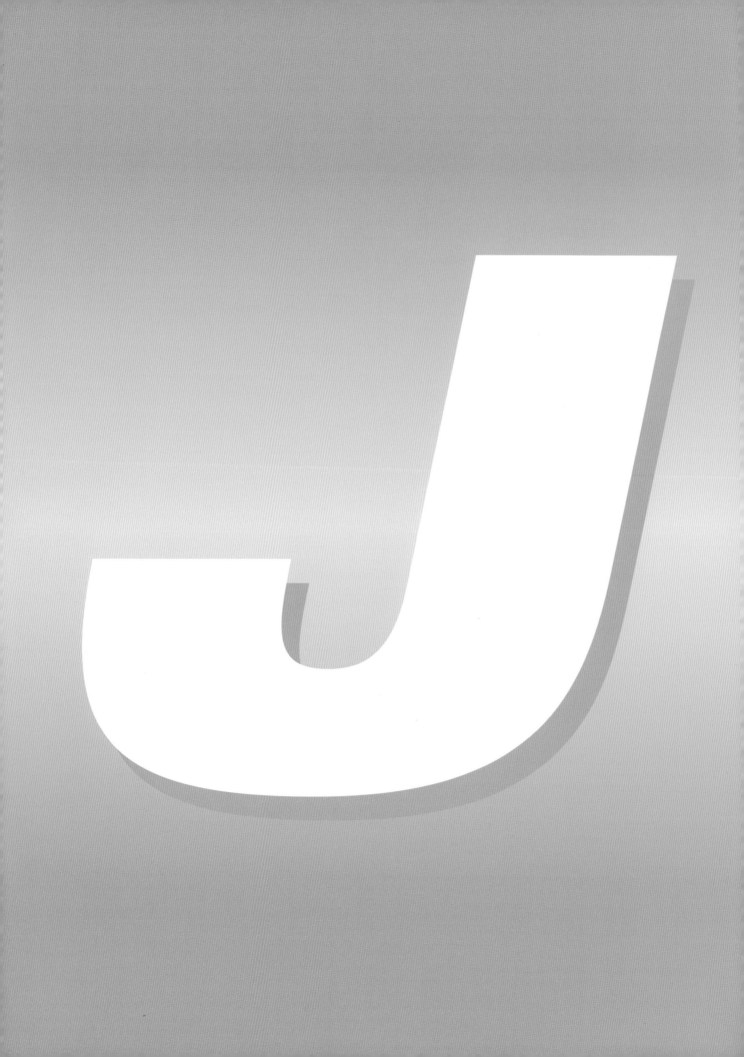

J

ASON 'J' BROWN is the Daddy of Five. Being the eldest (he's 23), J's taken on the role of band organizer – but that doesn't stop him from being the most in-yer-face member of the band. J is a typical Gemini – two people in one body! One minute he's the life and soul of the party, the next he's as quiet as a mouse.

Everyone will tell you he's intelligent and kind and can be a real gentleman – the kind of bloke who always holds the door open for a lady or gives up his seat on a train. He is also the most honourable man you will ever meet. But J has, as some might say, the shortest fuse in pop. Not one for biting his tongue, if he's antagonized or loses his cool, J can blow up and get mad veeerrrry quickly.

The mega-ambitious lad whose motto is 'Not if . . . When!' has been passionate about music since he was a toddler 'who never stopped singing'. Because of his dad's work in the forces, J, his mum Marilyn and sister Donna moved house 13 times in as many years. The family lived in Germany, Canada and all over

FACT FILE

Name: Jason Paul Brown

Date of birth: 13 June 1976

Star sign: Gemini

Height: 5' 10"

Place of birth: Aldershot, Hampshire

Hair colour: Brown

Eye colour: Blue

Previous jobs: Working in a warehouse

Fave sport: Football and weight-training

Hobbies: Music and women

Fave food: Chinese

Distinguishing features: Pierced eyebrow, short beard and facial scars

Family: Mum – Marilyn; Dad – Justin; Sister – Donna

One minute he's the life and soul of the party, the next he's as quiet as a mouse.

sky-diving J

J ON LOVE AND ROMANCE

'I'm very romantic and have been known to fill rooms with flowers for the lady in my life. My perfect romantic moment would be to take a girl to a Caribbean island, book into the penthouse of a luxury hotel and chill out in a massive four-poster bed for a couple of weeks. If I was seriously in love with my partner and we intended to stay together I'd give everything up for them. Nothing is more important than love. In fact, if I was forced to make the choice then I would die for love.'

Britain until they settled in Warrington where J cut his musical teeth, rapping with the band Prophets of Da Funk. After leaving college with nine GCSEs, J spent a year making demo-tapes of his solo work – until he joined Five and became a fully-fledged pop star.

With an eye for older women – he's been in a relationship with someone of 33 and wouldn't think twice about dating a lady in her forties! – J insists he can sniff a beautiful woman at 20 paces. But he's also been dubbed the 'king of chat' because he puts conversation way above looks in the love stakes.

So why don't we hear what J's got to say about himself ...

'I still can't believe how lucky I am to have realized my biggest ambition – to be in a band that's really successful – at such a young age. If somebody had said to me three years ago that I was going to be travelling the world in a band like Five, performing to hundreds of thousands of fans, I would have said, "Away with yer!" But here I am to tell the tale – and let me tell you, being in Five is cool!

'We are definitely going through the best times the band's ever had. At the end of 1998 things started going really wrong. We'd been working 18-hour days for months on end and it started to take its toll on us. After we did Australia and Japan we had to cancel going to Thailand because we were so mentally and physically hammered. It was a real disappointment missing the tour – I've always wanted to go to Thailand and meet the fans, so I hope we can go back soon.

'Having a break over Christmas with our families sorted us all out. We chilled and relaxed and then we did a promo tour of Argentina and

WHAT MAKES J CRY?

'I'm not one of those blokes who says, "Oh, I don't cry," because I can't see anything wrong with having a good cry. I don't cry easily, but I have shed a few tears over missing my mum and family. You don't realize how much you love your family until you move away from them. Scott and Abs see their families a lot 'cos they live around London, but I've only managed to see mine a couple of times since I've been in Five because they live miles away in Wales. I see them so rarely that when I have to say goodbye to them the tears start rolling.'

Me and Dad

everything just clicked into place – we all got so much closer. And me and Abs started getting on really well too. It wasn't that we hadn't got on before but when we started in the band there was a little bit of friction between us and occasionally we'd rub each other up the wrong way.

'We've all learned to live with each other and now we're so close we're like family to each other. A family united with one goal – to conquer the world as Five. It's been brilliant going round the world meeting our fans. There's no better feeling in the world than going to a country you've never visited and discovering that people are into the band.

'Our lifestyle has changed so much in the past year. I'm living in a really beautiful apartment with Sean now and there's nothing better than coming home and sitting on the balcony with a beer and relaxing. It was such a relief to leave the house we shared together – it was always in such a terrible mess and I like things to be tidy.

'We've also started to make a bit of money now, which is cool. When we started with the band we were on £100 per week. I haven't gone stupid with it and blown it on a BMW or something. None of us in the band are the kind of people –

J ON GIRLS

'I usually go for girls with dark hair and dark eyes. I've never been into blondes with blue eyes. I like women to have a bit of body and something to hold on to; there's nothing worse than skinny girls with biceps the size of my wrist. Any female in my life has to be sincere, honest and down to earth. And they have to be able to stimulate me with decent conversation. It's probably why I've always been into older women – they seem to be better conversationalists. You'd never see me with someone who's on TV or who's famous. I want to be with someone who is normal. I hate it when girls plaster themselves with make-up and then, when you see them in the morning without it, they look completely different. I don't see the point in trying to make yourself look different and pretend to be what you're not. It's false.'

J's FUTURE AMBITIONS

'I'm a very ambitious person and I want Five to be absolutely huge around the world. I also want to feel happy and content ... and busy. I'm one of those people who can't sit around doing nothing. I have to keep my mind active. Before I got into the band my biggest ambition was to be a solo artist, but now I want to be a producer some day. I don't think I'll want to perform after Five because I doubt anything would ever match the buzz. In the future I want to get a studio with Sean and work together as a production team. I'd like to settle down with a girl one day, but I don't want kids . . . well, not yet, anyway!'

It was such a relief to leave the house we shared together – it was always in such a terrible mess.

apart from Ritch who spends too much on clothes! – to waste money. Every now and then I might treat myself to a watch, or something electrical – but I'm careful. It's brilliant to know that I have some financial security and I'm not going to blow it.

'I think I've changed since being in Five. I've become more confident about a lot of things. When we started out it was the big question: "Is the band going to be successful?" Now I know things have gone well I've relaxed a bit. I used to be so stressed out that I was always on guard and would attack people straight away if I didn't agree with them. I've now learned that talking works much better than shouting – especially if you can agree to disagree.

'I had a real breakthrough about myself when I was in the shower last night. I suddenly realized that I can't expect to have something from someone if I'm not prepared to give back the same. I hope I'm going somewhere in my head that's a lot better. I still lose it and scream and shout and break things – and then regret it. But I've chilled a lot and it's much better for me because I'm less frustrated. And I bet the rest of the band agree that it's better for them too!'

My new best friend!

Lights, camera, action!

Five on the Road

I N THEIR quest to conquer the world, Five have visited more countries than most people see in a lifetime! In the past two years Sean, J, Ritchie, Scott and Abs have lived like supersonic travellers, spending more time in planes, airports, Duty Free lounges, limousines and hotel rooms than in their own homes.

Along the way they have met millions of new fans and notched up countless golden memories. Undoubtedly, the experiences the lads have shared – as Five's incredible success has unfolded around the world – will unite them for ever. So what are the amazing stories that, one day, Ritchie, Abs, Scott, J and Sean will recite to their own kids?

Here we find out about that – and so much more! – as they describe the highs and the lows of life on the road with Five...

IN THE AIR

J: I'd love to know just how many air-miles we've clocked up over the past two years.
SEAN: It's got to be over a million – if not two!

J: It's funny how everybody has developed their own travelling habits. Ritchie sits there looking out the window at the clouds, daydreaming in a world of his own. Sean and me tuck into some bevies, watch a few films or mess about. Scott always moans because he's had to get out of bed

Airport madness!

Don't forget to wake us up

Scott and fans

Just chillin'

Ritchie sits there looking out the window at the clouds, daydreaming in a world of his own.

Let's just say he wasn't the most popular member of the band that day!

too early. As soon as we get on a plane, Scott's asleep before we've even taxied to the runway. He only wakes up when the wheels touch down!

SCOTT: That's not exactly true! I do stay awake sometimes! The last time we came back from America I listened to Phil Collins on my Discman and wrote a letter on my lap-top!

RITCHIE: I read and Abs reads occasionally; the others don't. I love the author Irvine Welsh and have been reading *Ecstasy* and *Filth*. I like long-haul flights now that we travel First Class – there's so much more room and you get all the top movies. I know I sound completely geriatric, but I love puzzle books and always do them on the plane.

J: Ritchie is a geriatric sometimes! He always forgets things – if it's not his watch or his bags it'll be his passport. He left his passport on the plane coming home from Spain; it took hours to get somebody to check the plane and find it. We were hanging around for hours. Let's just say

he wasn't the most popular member of the band that day!

SEAN: Me, J, Abs and Rob have fights in the middle of the plane. They threatened to kick us off when we came back from Ireland because we were getting too out of hand.

ABS: Remember that time when we got that dirty joke book out of *FHM* magazine when we were in America? We were telling jokes out of it for hours. Some of them were soooo obscene!

J: We fly Business or First Class now and people

Abs

Sean

I get guilt trips about having money because there's so many people who don't have any.

in those sections don't like it when Five are on board. We used to muck around on purpose to wind people up, but now we've changed. We're much more respectful of other people.

ABS: Yeah, we have changed a lot actually. We're much better behaved. Ritchie always puts money into the charity envelope you get in the back of your seat – he put $80 in last time!

RITCHIE: The lads thought I was mad, but I wanted to do it because I could. I get guilt trips about having money because there's so many people who don't have any.

SEAN: We have been delayed on so many flights – and it's always when we're on the way home. We never get delayed if we're working. When we were still flying economy we once spent five hours on the runway in New York. They kept saying we were going to take off, but we'd taxi round the runway for half an hour, stop and then do it all over again. It was like a spoof movie. It went on for five hours and they wouldn't give us any food or drink because they wanted to save it for the flight!

SCOTT: We used to clap every time the plane landed and give the pilot marks out of 10. If it was a bad landing we'd shout out 'Whoooah! Bad

Scott

Ritchie

One thing you can always say about Five – we always smell good!

landing!' really loudly. Once in America the pilot made a terrible landing and we were shouting out: 'Dodgy landing, mate – you only got 3 out of 10 for that.' His door was open and the captain came out and started screaming at us: 'If you think you can land it better than that buddy, you try and land it.' He was so mad at us, but the more he shouted the more we laughed!

ON THE GROUND

SCOTT: If we've spent millions of hours in the air, we must have spent billions in airport terminals around the world.

ABS: The shop Dixons in Duty Free must love Five. We always buy loads of things. I can't believe they're going to abolish Duty Free – what will we do??!!

RITCHIE: Either myself or J spend the most in Duty Free. J's really into aftershave and is always buying new ones. I think he almost has one for every day now. I'm into Dolce & Gabbana and J.P. Gaultier, Scott's into Bulgari and J's just got into Chanel's Allure For Men. One thing you can always say about Five – we always smell good!

ABS: The best airport lounge in the world has to be the Virgin Airlines Lounge in London. It's got free arcade games, free hot food and drinks and free telephone calls to anywhere in the world. My mum met Richard Branson in the lounge the last time we flew Virgin – and got her photo taken with him. She was made up!

J: I love the things you see and the people you meet when you're travelling. And, because we're all loony, we always have a laugh. I'll never forget when Abs sat on the luggage carousel when we came back from America. He was sitting in amongst all these suitcases going round and round for ages – until this security bloke spotted him and went mad!

HOTELS AROUND THE WORLD

RITCHIE: I'm sure hotels think Five are all completely mad. When we go down to eat in the restaurant we order practically everything on the menu. The waiters wheel in four trolleys of food, looking at us as if we're nutters. It sounds really pretentious and wasteful, but it is a laugh.

ABS: The thing is, we still can't believe that we get to stay in some of the best hotels in the world. Some of them are so luxurious, it's like something out of a Bond movie!

SCOTT: We used to share hotel rooms, but we all have our own these days. Usually I'll just

listen to music, watch films or occasionally write music. But most of my time I spend on the phone to my friends and family back home.

RITCHIE: We have the biggest phone bills. In fact they are so huge they're too obscene to print! I like my space and I really enjoy just chilling out in my room after work. Sometimes I'll go out to a restaurant to eat, but most of the time I try to get an early night. All the fans are going to think I'm really boring, but I prefer to get an early night if I'm working the next day. I hate working if I'm tired because I get all moody and can't concentrate.

SCOTT: Sean goes clubbing the most. If anybody's going out you can guarantee it's Sean.

RITCHIE: I had a conversation with J the other day because I was worried that the rest of the lads would think I didn't like them any more because I don't go out with them much in the evening. It's just that if I do go out to a club I spend my whole time wishing I was somewhere else being mentally stimulated. When I joined the band I was a complete club freak; my bedroom walls were covered with club flyers. But I don't like going to clubs any more. Put it this way, I've danced the night away to death. I'd prefer to have a good conversation than go clubbing.

Another airport bus

Another dressing room

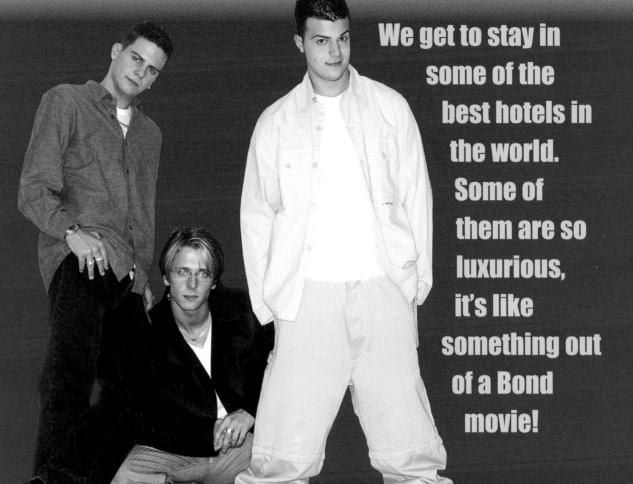

We get to stay in some of the best hotels in the world. Some of them are so luxurious, it's like something out of a Bond movie!

ABS: Me and J play loads of practical jokes. We sneak into each other's rooms and tip the beds up and mess everything up – or put something gross, like a bit of old sandwich, under the sheets, so when someone gets into bed they get a shock!

RITCHIE: Sean is the most difficult to wake up in the morning. Probably because he's always out late. You could jump on his head and he'll still stay asleep!

SEAN: You can talk! You're always late in the mornings when we have to leave.

J: You wouldn't believe the number of times either me or Rob have had to break into Ritchie's room to wake him up. And then pack his bag for him so we don't miss our flight. He's always at least 45 minutes late!

Abs takes a snack

Sean goes clubbing the most. If anybody's going out you can guarantee it's Sean.

RITCHIE: I remember once waking up in America and Rob was at the end of my bed screaming at me! I nearly had a heart-attack. He'd broken into my room because nobody could wake me up. They'd been phoning and hammering on the door and I slept through it. We were going to miss our flight so Rob chucked my stuff into my case while I got dressed. We made it just in time!

ABS: Yeah, thanks to Rob!

BACKSTAGE WITH FIVE

J: We all have different ways of getting ourselves psyched up for a performance.

ABS: Yeah, it's a real private moment for the band when we're getting ready in the dressing room.

RITCHIE: Abs throws food around and goes all hyperactive.

SEAN: I like just chilling until it's time to go on stage.

Travelling through Holland

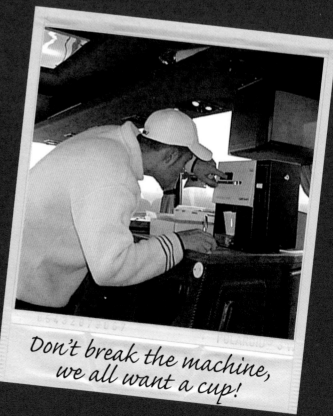

Don't break the machine, we all want a cup!

SCOTT: Ritchie and me like to have a few minutes to ourselves before we go on.

RITCHIE: Then we all have a ritual where the five of us stand in a circle, put our hands on top of each other's and chant: 'Five – what you waiting 4 – if you wanna – 3 – 3 – 2 – 2 – 1 – let's do it!'

FIVE ON THE ROAD

SCOTT: When we're in England, my dad and Rob drive us around in Previa vans with blacked-out windows. My dad has converted a bed in the back of our Previa and sometimes we are so tired that we all fall asleep snuggled into each other.

ABS: Once we were in the Prev, driving near Richmond, and I was being really silly hanging out of the sliding door. Suddenly these police officers stopped us and went mad – luckily they were called off to an emergency otherwise we would have been in deep trouble!

RITCHIE: It's really funny if Rob gets annoyed and shouts at other drivers. Sometimes they come up to the car looking for aggro – but as soon as they lay eyes on Rob and see how big he is they just go away!

J: We've had some really scary drivers abroad. We were in Holland and were running so late that we were sure we were going to miss our flight. This guy who was driving us was a nutcase. We were getting thrown from one side of the car to the other and had about 10 near-miss accidents. We were praying for our lives. But we have to hand it to the bloke – he got us there on time!

SEAN: We nearly got killed in Dublin. A car pulled straight out of a junction at us. We would have had a head-on collision if the driver hadn't slammed his brakes on. He saved our lives. We'd just like to say: 'Thank you, mate!'

J: We nearly had a terrible crash with our manager Chris once. We had to swerve to miss another car. It was a really close shave. Scott was sitting in the back and all he was worried about was the fact that he'd spilled the chips he was eating on the floor!

SEAN: J is very funny. He's got the most brilliant sense of humour and is a fantastic mimic. In the bus he does all these hilarious sketches – usually with Abs. They do funny voices and play different characters. The best ones are their schoolboys and nerd sketches – a right laugh!

KDWL show, USA

T WAS bound to happen! As soon as Five's special brand of breathtaking talent was unleashed across the Atlantic they took America by storm, ripping up all the record books in their wake. They racked up a Top 10 in the prestigious Billboard Hot 100 Chart with 'When The Lights Go Out' and watched their debut album *Five* reach No.1 in the Heatseekers Chart and go platinum. And, to top it all, Five have now proved to be the most successful British male band in America since the Bay City Rollers in the 1970s!

After a blitzing 1998 promotional tour that took in virtually every radio station, shopping mall and football stadium across the country, Five spent the whole of last summer playing radio festivals and delivering spine-tingling live performances in front of ecstatic 40,000-strong audiences.

Soon the name Five was on the lips of every mover and shaker in the music business and before long the band came to the attention of two great American institutions – Disney and Pepsi. The soft drinks giant offered to become Five's official 1999 sponsors – much to the Pepsi-drinking lads' joy! – and enrolled them on their latest advertising campaign with the likes of Janet Jackson. Disney signed the lads up to appear in the Disney Channel's 'In Concert' special with B*Witched, which featured performance footage of the lads together with exclusive behind-the-scenes interviews – and brought them to the attention of a billion more viewers worldwide.

With a start like that, what else can Five say but: 'America, here we come!'

J: I just can't believe we have been accepted in America. Personally, I never thought Five would make it out there. I was knocked out when we were told that Five is the first British band that's been so successful since the Bay City Rollers! And that was in the 1970s – before most of us were even born. It's just amazing to think I'm in a band that's successful in America when groups like Take That never cracked it and Boyzone are still trying.

Hollywood here we come...

J: One of the maddest places we've visited is Argentina. There are always thousands of fans outside the hotel. You open the window and it sounds like a football crowd chanting. Every time we left the hotel there'd be hundreds of fans following us in taxis – sitting on the roof, hanging out the windows. I remember the day that was a turning point for me with Five, when I realized – probably for the first time – that we had made a success of the band. We went to do a studio performance at the biggest radio station in Buenos Aires, but the studio was too small. There were so many fans outside they had to shut off the whole street. The police wouldn't give us clearance to perform on the street because of the crowd, but we didn't want to disappoint our fans. So we drove up in front of the radio station, lifted out the skylight on the bus and climbed out. We performed three numbers before the police shut us down.

Five have now proved to be the most successful British male band in America since the Bay City Rollers in the 1970s!

Disneyland

SEAN: The Disney Special we filmed was the most amazing thing we've done with Five. We performed on this amazing stage surrounded by fairy-lights and stars – just like something out of a movie. The crowd went wild – they were queuing around the block for our autographs.
RITCHIE: And it was great working with the girls from B*Witched. They are such lovely girls – me and Scott love them, don't we?
SCOTT: Yeah!
SEAN: In DisneyWorld, we stayed in a hotel where Abs got a Mickey Mouse voice wake-up call in the morning.

ABS: It completely freaked me out!

SCOTT: We travel so much and stay in so many different hotels – literally hundreds of them! – that we can end up not knowing where we are in the world. When we were doing the Disney Special I woke up in this king-size bed and couldn't find the lights. I was scrabbling around and then I found them. I thought I was in my bed at home and when I put the lights on I freaked out. All I could see was Mickey Mouse curtains.

J: It was brilliant going to the theme park, but it was really embarrassing when we were being filmed on the rides. We jumped the queue every time and were walking past people who were on paid holidays and had been waiting for over two hours. I felt so uncomfortable. But people were really nice about it and didn't seem to mind at all. We went on this ride where you go up 13 storeys in an elevator – it stops and the door opens, and then suddenly you plunge to the bottom.

SEAN: We had several goes and loved it. But our American stylist Dave freaked out and started screaming that he wanted to get off.

RITCHIE: Disney were really nice and gave us some money to go shopping in

SCOTT: It was so funny when we went to Orlando for some promo work. Me, Abs and Ritchie walked through passport control and this bloke came over and asked what we were doing there. I told him we'd come to promote our latest single, but he tried to send us home because our visas had run out. We knew it was okay because we weren't doing paid work, just promotions, so we didn't need a visa – but he was having none of it. We were in this room for two hours, being grilled like we were desperate criminals. He even gave us tickets home and told us we were going on the next flight back. We ended up having a fit of the giggles. But it was okay in the end; the record company sorted it out and they let us in the country. I'm sure the bloke was very disappointed, though. He was itching to send us home.

Quick, I'm getting wet . . .

Hard Rockers

Sometimes we'd catch three planes and visit three different states in a day!

I didn't mean to do it . . .

It's just amazing to think I'm in a band that's successful in America when groups like Take That never cracked it and Boyzone are still trying.

Melrose, near where we were staying. There were some brilliant shops and we were running from shop to shop buying sunglasses, music, clothes – everything we could get our hands on. We could never do it in Oxford Street, so it was a real novelty.

SCOTT: We've literally travelled across America several times. Sometimes we'd catch three planes and visit three different states in a day! You can guarantee that if anything happens to make us late, it only happens when we've got time off. If we're working, then everything goes like clockwork. Once in America, we had a day off and were flying back to Los Angeles. We were just about to take off and an eagle flew into the plane's engine. Our flight ended up being delayed for eight hours. We were more worried about missing time off than the fact that we hadn't crashed and died!

RITCHIE: What about all the trouble we've had with missing luggage! We had a terrible time getting to Memphis. We missed a connecting flight and my luggage went missing. Everybody else got their bags apart from me! I only had the clothes I'd been wearing for two days, travelling – and I didn't want to have to wear them on stage!

Hollywood

Smash Hits magazine were coming out to see the show and lots of US TV stations were filming us. I'd have looked a right prat in my old trackie bottoms! In the end our press officers, Heather and Emma, went dashing out with Rob to buy me some clothes – they only had half an hour before the shops shut! They were brilliant and got me some good clothes. But I admit, I was worrying a bit!

SCOTT: Yeah, you drunk all our cans of Pepsi while you were pacing up and down waiting for Heather and Emma to arrive.

SEAN: It was a shame we weren't doing our Pepsi ad-campaign shoot – there would have been more than enough cans around to keep even Ritchie happy!

ABS: We've performed in some brilliant places. In New York we did a gig in front of 10,000 people in Times Square. That was wicked! Then we went to an old bowling alley in Brooklyn to shoot the US video for 'When The Lights Go Out'. We all had a go bowling and got very competitive with each other!

SEAN: When I first went to New York I was a bit scared. Not because I thought I was going to get shot or anything, but because it was so manic and noisy with taxis beeping their horns non-stop. It's like nowhere else in the world.

The Disneyland bus

Graceland awaits

RITCHIE: When we went to Memphis I kept going on about wanting to visit Graceland. We didn't have enough time for a proper visit so I persuaded the lads that we should at least go and take some pictures. We were in this enormous, white stretch limo and when we pulled up outside the gates the security guard was very nice and accommodating. He opened the security gates for us so we could go in and take pictures of us kissing the tarmac. We started trying to climb over the wall into the hangar where the planes were kept, but thought twice about it in case we got shot for trespassing or something. We stopped to take more pictures outside the Graceland sign which was all lit up, but within seconds we started getting attacked by all these flying bugs. They were disgusting – absolutely enormous. So we all jumped back in the limo, quick!

J: I have a problem with cities when they're dirty, noisy, polluted and overcrowded. They're always so impersonal. The last time we went I was walking down the street and moved out of the way to let an old lady pass. When she walked past she was watching my every move as if she thought I was going to rob her or something. I was only trying to be polite.

So relaxed

Got the feelin'

So we drove up in front of the radio station, lifted out the skylight on the bus and climbed out. We performed three numbers before the police shut us down.

SEAN: It was mad when we went to re-shoot the video of 'It's The Things You Do' for the US. We filmed in California on this massive racetrack in the desert. There were stunt cars and drivers jumping over hay bales and crashing into things. I knew the desert would be hot, but I wasn't prepared for the temperatures under the lights – boiling! It was exciting, but we had to get up so early every day and I'm really not a morning person. Because the sun goes down in the desert at about 5 p.m., and we were doing a daylight shoot, we had to be on set at 4.30 a.m. every day! I mean, 4.30 a.m. – that's the time when I'm normally coming home – not getting up!

SEAN: New York's very interesting, but I wouldn't want to have to try and survive there if I didn't have any money. It must be very tough.
J: That's it, everyone's surviving and nobody's just chilling. I like LA 'cos everything's more chilled and there's always a great view from the hotel where we stay on Sunset. It's a totally different lifestyle to New York, like it's another country. A lot of it's superficial in LA but there's a lot more space. The weather's great so you can swim and sunbathe.
ABS: Remember when we saw the Hollywood sign for the first time? I was like: 'Wow!'
SCOTT: We had a brilliant time when all our families came out to stay in LA for a mini-holiday. It was great for them to see us working – now they know that we're not exaggerating when we say it's hard work!
RITCHIE: I love Florida and LA because they're so sunny – give me a pool and I'm happy! We still haven't been to San Francisco, and I'm dying to get there because I'm sure I'd really love it. New York is really cool for shopping, but it gets a bit mad if you're there for a long time. I've realized that I'm a country bumpkin at heart – cities aren't really my thing.
ABS: We did some incredible festivals in America. In Oregon we did a show to 40,000 people in a field one afternoon – it was like performing at Glastonbury!

Big dipper

The shopaholics!

I really wanted to ask him if I could come on the show but I was too embarrassed and lost my nerve.

J: It was great to have a chance to prove ourselves. In America you always perform live – they don't do playbacks there – so you're judged on your true ability, not just on the records. We were performing live to 30,000 people in football stadiums and 5,000 people a time in shopping malls all over the country. It was a fantastic time because we love performing best of all.

SEAN: I liked Orlando, the weather and the vibe, but we didn't get enough time to explore the place.

J: That's the biggest disappointment about being in a group. You travel to all these amazing places in the world, but never get enough time to see them. The most we see of places is when we transfer from the hotel to the airport and vice versa. We never saw enough of Washington, Houston, Seattle or Portland.

SEAN: Tennessee was really chilled out though!

J: I remember that night. We were meant to be playing a venue in a bit of a rough area and we were concerned it wouldn't go well. We only agreed to go on when we saw there were all these beautiful women out in the audience.

ABS: People always treated us well in America. And the fans were mad . . . brilliantly mad! And that's what we love because that's where we get our energy from.

ABS: LA is the place to spot stars. You can literally walk down the street and see people like Pamela Anderson and Cindy Crawford sitting outside cafés. It's also the place where you can bump into the strangest people – people you'd never expect in a million years to see there. We were filming in a café for a TV special and out of the corner of my eye I spotted Greg Proops from the TV improvisation show *Whose Line Is It Anyway?* I was like: 'Yeah! I watch *Whose Line Is It Anyway?* all the time!' We had a long chat while he was in the café having a snack with his family. I really wanted to ask him if I could come on the show – I love doing improvisation – but I was too embarrassed and lost my nerve. I hope he's reading this – maybe he'll invite me on the show soon!

Sean

SEAN KEIRAN CONLON is Baby Five. He may be the youngest member in the band (he's 18!) but he's also the tallest – six feet at the last check and growing fast! Sean is probably the most private person on the planet and definitely the most laid-back. He's very quiet (a listener and thinker rather than a talker) but get him on a subject he's interested in – as long as it's not himself! – and he'll go on for hours. Sean very rarely opens up or talks about the way he feels. But he has very strong opinions and can be exceedingly stubborn.

He's best described as a professional northerner, with a dry-as-a-bone sense of humour to match. But scratch beneath the surface and what you find is a seriously kind and gentle bloke who always looks out for people less fortunate than himself. If you pass a homeless person on the street, Sean's the one who goes back to make sure he's okay and buy him a cup of coffee. And when he plays with his little sister, Charlotte, and you see how much they adore each other, it's impossible not to notice his loving, sensitive side.

sean taking a break

FACT FILE

Name: Sean Keiran Conlon

Date of birth: 20 May 1981

Star sign: Taurus

Height: 6' – and still growing!

Place of birth: Leeds

Hair colour: Black

Eye colour: Brown

Previous jobs: House removals

Fave sport: Rugby League

Hobbies: Music and ladies

Fave food: Pasta

Distinguishing features: Shaven head

Family: Mum – Kate; Dad – Dennis;
Sisters – Charlotte and Katrina;
Half-brothers – John and Dominic

Even as a kid, Sean would save up his school-dinner money all week to buy a girl a present. He grew up in a close-knit family in Leeds with his mum, Kate, sisters Charlotte and Katrina and half-brothers Dominic and John. The family lived just around the corner from Scary Spice, Mel B – who Sean admits was scary even back then! His parents split when he was nine and his dad Dennis now lives in Southport, Lancashire.

Despite his young age, Sean is a major talent. He's been singing since he was four, had his first recording session at 11 and won the Yamaha Young Composer competition when he was only 13. So it came as no surprise that he won his place in Five when he was still at school!

He may not be the chattiest man in pop, but people always have something to say about him. So why don't we listen up to something very rare – what Sean's got to say about himself!

'The best things about being in Five are travelling, recording in the studio with top-class producers and performing. Everything in fact! I can't believe that I'm only 18 and I've been to dozens of countries around the world performing our own songs to thousands of fans! I spent my

SEAN ON LOVE AND ROMANCE

'If I was completely in love with someone I'd do anything for them. There are absolutely no limits when you're in love. In some ways, love is the best feeling in the world. But there are downsides – you can get very hurt when things go wrong. Girls always seem to think I'm this real hard person with no soft side, but I do have my soppy moments – honest! The trouble is, it's hard to know if a girl likes you for yourself or because you're in a band. I met a girl in Tunisia before I got into Five, but I kept ringing her up and it was no go. As soon as she heard I'd got into Five she rang up, so I said: "Hop it. Away with yer." She shouldn't phone just because I'm in a band. All of us in Five talk about women and relationships, but apart from Abs nobody has really had a girlfriend since we've been in the band. I'd love a girlfriend, but you can't make it happen by clicking your fingers – you have to meet them first!'

Me, Dad and my little bro at
the Rugby League final

childhood dreaming about being in the music industry.

'This year has been the best in Five so far. We've really gelled as a band and learned to cope more with the pressures. It was very difficult for us last year – we'd been abroad on the road for months and started to fall like flies. We all started to get ill and stressed because we were having a massive lack of sleep every day and weren't having enough healthy food.

'Rob our tour manager – who used to be a professional footballer – has helped us all to learn to cope with stress. He teaches us T'ai Chi and breathing exercises and makes sure we keep fit by coaching us for our Five five-a-side football team. If you're in tune with your body you're in tune with your mind. The most important thing is to keep calm, even if everything's going mad around you. If I'm feeling wound up I take a deep breath, hold it for seven seconds, and then breathe out for eight seconds – and repeat it four times. It really works!

'I've changed and grown up a lot since joining the band because I've experienced things that most lads of my age never get a chance to see or

Ben does the daily shave

SEAN ON GIRLS

'I don't really look for anything in particular when it comes to girls. You don't know who's going to be the ideal girl for you until you meet them. You might have an idea in your mind of the person you'd like to meet – but you're never going to find someone to live up to that ideal because, at the end of the day, it's only a dream in your head. You know, I think I'm the only bloke I know who's never had a poster of a woman on my wall. I do like nice eyes and nice smiles, but the qualities I like in a girl are far more important than what she looks like. If I'm having a night out, the girl I'll notice will be dead plain, reserved but confident and giving off an air of being dead genuine. But there's not much chance of me chatting her up. I'm always so laid-back. It's not that I'm shy – I just don't like coming on to girls.'

If you're in tune with your body you're in tune with your mind. The most important thing is to keep calm, even if everything's going mad around you.

WHAT MAKES SEAN CRY?

'I find it hard to cry nowadays. When I was younger I used to cry a lot, but now I can't get it out. The last time I cried was at Christmas when I was over-tired, but it wasn't proper crying.'

It's made me even more laid-back – if that's possible!

Of course, I'm dead flattered if somebody wants my autograph.

SEAN'S FUTURE AMBITIONS

'I'm not too sure yet. To be honest, I'm pretty happy with the way things are going now. There isn't much I'd want to change. I'm having the time of my life, travelling and performing all over the world. When I was 11, I started searching for a record deal. Now I have one and I'm doing what I always wanted to do! What could be better than that? One thing I would really like to do is set my family up for life. And I'd like to get married one day – but not for years yet! I am only 18!'

do. It's made me even more laid-back – if that's possible! If something bothers me now, I'm much more relaxed about it. I don't go after aggro and always keep my cool.

'I'm not really a business kind of bloke but I've had to get more of a business head on me since being in Five. I mean, I didn't even have a bank account when I was in Leeds and now I've got an accountant and a lawyer and all that sort of stuff that comes with being in the music business.

'Having money has given me a lot more freedom. If I want to go for a drink or go out for something to eat I don't have to think: 'Have I got a tenner in my pocket? Can I afford it?' But I am careful with my money. I want to make sure I set myself up for the future and I won't be able to do that if I'm spending all the time. The only thing I've bought myself since being in the band is a camera, so I can record all my memories of being in Five.

'Even though being in Five is brilliant, there are downsides to being famous if you're quiet like me. Of course, I'm dead flattered if somebody wants my autograph. But I still get a bit embarrassed when I get recognised – it's just not me being the centre of attention.'

I'm still waiting

FIVE HAVE racked up plenty of serious chart success in Australia – the album, *Five*, has gone platinum a staggering three times! But despite the phenomenal record sales, nobody was prepared for the fantastic response the lads received when they went Down Under for the first time last year.

As soon as they stepped off the plane and were greeted by thousands of ecstatic Aussie fans, Five knew they were in for a whirlwind promo tour with a difference. They were booked to appear on the top pop show *Hey! Hey! It's Saturday!*, perform at Sydney and Melbourne's largest shopping malls, record dozens of radio and press interviews and appear at countless signing venues. But in between their manic schedule Five soon discovered that they couldn't leave their hotel rooms without being mobbed...

J: The fans in Australia were wicked!

SEAN: Yeah. We were so taken aback by the response we got from the fans. It was mad! We were all really tired, but wherever we went the fans were there supporting us. They kept us going and made us feel like the hard work was worth it.

SCOTT: I remember sitting in my hotel room, looking out at the beautiful view. I was really missing home, so I put on the instrumental version of Titanic and leaned over the balcony. When I saw all the fans out there I felt so touched that I started crying my eyes out.

RITCHIE: As soon as we arrived I thought: 'Yeah, I could live here!' All the people were so, so friendly. It's the sort of place where everybody says hello to each other in the street. It's a really nice friendly touch. Not like other countries where they look at you as if you're completely bonkers if you say hello to someone you don't know!

J: When I was a kid, Australia seemed a million miles away – the sort of place you see on TV. I never thought I'd actually ever get to go there. It was brilliant when we arrived and drove past famous landmarks like the Sydney Opera House – the only disappointing thing was that we passed it at 60 mph and weren't able to stop and have a proper look because our schedule was so tight.

ABS: Yeah. I was gutted we didn't have any time off because I've got family there and I would have loved to have seen them. Australia feels like home to me because I used to spend holidays in

Where's the bus?

Take it away, Abs!

RITCHIE: 'I had the weirdest and most coincidental experience in Melbourne. We were on stage, in the middle of performing 'Slam!' when I suddenly spotted two people in the 5,000-strong audience I went to school with. I was so surprised I nearly fell over. I was like: "No way!" They were screaming "Ritchie! Ritchie!" and waving at me like lunatics. We met up after the show and it turned out that they were travelling the world. They'd gone past a record shop earlier in the day where we were doing a signing, looked in and saw the Five posters. They couldn't believe it! So they asked where we were going to be that night and turned up. After the show we had a few drinks and went clubbing. It was a mad night. I didn't come home until about 10 a.m.!'

signing in Melbourne

Melbourne when I was a kid. We'd go fishing and play golf every day. I like the outdoors way of life there, it's really chilled. It's such a shame we didn't have more time. I really wanted to go to Ayres Rock.

J: And Bondi beach!

SEAN: J only wanted to go to the beach so he could check out the girls!

J: What red-blooded male wouldn't want to go to Bondi beach and see the girls? They're meant to be among the best-looking women in the world!

SCOTT: I'd really like to go back to Australia. The spaghetti bolognese was brilliant. The best I've had anywhere in the world!

ABS: And you get the best passion fruit ice-cream too!

When I saw all the fans out there I felt so touched that I started crying my eyes out.

SCOTT: Australia was where I had huge problems with my hair! Don't laugh, it was really serious! I've always spent hours on my hair to make sure it's just right. To get the look I wanted I used bucket-loads of styling products like gel and wax. The trouble is my head got to the point where it had had enough. I'd been using so much product that my scalp started to bleed. It was covered in painful, red, weeping sores. We had to get a special trichologist in to have a look at my scalp and even he was shocked at the state of it. He gave me strict instructions not to wash my hair or do anything to it for at least a week. Ugh! I had to wear a cap for a whole week, so nobody could see what a state my hair was in!

SEAN: We performed on Australia's biggest pop show *Hey! Hey! It's Saturday!* when we were in Melbourne. It was such a buzz! We met this brilliant bloke called Molly Moldrom, the star presenter who is a right laugh. He wears these trademark cowboy hats and boots. He invited us to dinner at his house which was the most beautiful place I've been inside in my life. He even had a fish pond in the garden. The food and wine was fantastic – I wish I had dinners like that at home!

RITCHIE: We had some really funny moments because we were so tired and delirious from lack of sleep. When we arrived in Melbourne for a promotion Scott grabbed the microphone and started singing Frank Sinatra's song 'Let There Be Love'. The audience clapped thinking he was doing an a cappella number. He wasn't – he'd just gone bonkers!

SCOTT: Rob our tour manager sent me home. He told me to go back to the hotel because I was embarrassing myself. Not for the first time!

ABS: I can't wait to go back to Australia. It's the first place I'm going to visit for a holiday when we get some time off from the band.

SCOTT, RITCHIE, SEAN and J: Yeah. Me too!

Who's next?

J: We'd been on the road for a solid year without one day off – and we were all falling to pieces. To be honest, I'd got to the stage where I didn't think I could carry on any longer. I remember we did this in-store signing and I was so tired I could hardly keep my eyes open. As soon as we walked in there was this enormous roar from the fans. It was so loud I had to cover my ears with my hands. The fans were so friendly and gave us the most beautiful presents and letters. Everybody was so nice to us and gave us such a brilliant reception. To be honest we were so made up that we had a bit of a cry on the way back to the hotel!

I'd really like to go back to Australia. The spaghetti bolognese was brilliant.

Hi girls!

We'd been on the road for a solid year without one day off – and we were all falling to pieces.

ABS: They've got to be some of the best fans in the world. We did a performance at a shopping mall and there were over 5,000 girls there. When we finished the crowds were so mad we had to be escorted out by about 50 security guards – they literally had to form this human shield around us. It was the weirdest experience of my life – I couldn't decide whether I felt like a president or a pop star!

Bit classy, these limos

Ritchie

rICHARD NEVILLE is the sensitive member of Five – you can tell what he's thinking just by looking at his face – but he's still one of the lads! Ritchie is a people's person. He's warm and friendly and easy to talk to, which makes him perfect for his role as Five's peacemaker. If there's ever any falling out between the lads you can guarantee Ritchie is there smoothing over the aggro with his catchphrase: 'Hey, guys, c'mon – chill out and be friends!'

A thinker, who's always got his nose in a book, Ritchie is also a terrible worrier – he's been known to worry about what might happen in five years' time! He's also the most romantic in the band – and writes poems and love songs for the lady in his life.

Everybody says that Ritchie is just like his mum Kim, who's also chatty, warm and funny. Born in Solihull, Birmingham, Ritchie is the baby of the

FACT FILE

Name: Ritchie – Richard Neville

Date of birth: 23 August 1979

Star sign: Leo

Height: 5' 9"

Place of birth: Birmingham

Hair colour: Brown

Eye colour: Blue

Previous jobs: Worked in a burger van and in his mum's pub

Fave sport: Football and rugby

Hobbies: Music and ladies

Fave food: Chinese and side breast of chicken in KFC

Distinguishing features: Twinkling baby blue eyes

Family: Mum – Kim: Dad – Peter; Stepdad – Derek: Elder sister – Tracey; Elder brother – Dave

Los Angeles at my feet

Performing is more important to me than materialistic things.

family. His mum split with dad Peter when Ritchie was two and later married Derek. With his elder sister Tracey and brother Dave, Ritchie spent much of his childhood in the Crab Mill pub in Bromsgrove – only because their mum Kim and stepdad Derek are landlords.

Ritchie's parents struggled to send him to the posh public school in Bromsgrove – where he worked long hours, six days a week! He later discovered he had dyslexia, which he says accounts for his love of music and acting over academic work. He was in a band at school and quickly built up a large following of female fans who fell in love with his big smile and electric-blue eyes. With his obvious good looks and raging acting talent, it wasn't long before he was snapped up by the famous National Youth Theatre. But he put his acting ambitions on hold after winning his place in Five.

Let's listen to what one of the easiest members of Five has got to say...

'It's been hard work travelling and working almost every day for the past two years with the band, but it has paid off. It's a really good feeling to know I've worked my arse off and got somewhere. Just a year ago the band were living together in the house. It was a pigsty and I was lonely and

RITCHIE ON LOVE AND ROMANCE

'When I'm in love my heart skips a beat, I get butterflies in my stomach and find it hard to eat anything. I'm a really soppy person when I'm in love, always writing poems and love songs. Romance is very important to me – and my idea of the perfect romantic evening is relaxing in my flat with the girl I love, just the two of us. I'm a very demanding boyfriend and need fulfilment emotionally. I need to be told I'm loved and want 100 percent devotion. In fact I'm quite possessive. You could never call me a cool boyfriend – I'd rather be called interesting!'

really needed a girlfriend. Now I've got an apartment I'm really happy. It makes me feel good having a home to go back to. I must sound so boring, but I'm quite a hermit when I've got time off. I like staying in my flat watching videos and having close friends round to chill out and relax.

'Since being in Five I've realised that it's the job I get a kick out of. I like working on something and making it good and then showing people. It might sound

Whaddya think?

But we wouldn't be where we are without the fans. Seeing their faces light up with excitement and pleasure about what we do is the best feeling in the world.

egotistical, but performing is more important to me than materialistic things. Lots of people moan that fame means you don't have a private life. In a funny sort of sadistic way I don't mind not having any privacy. I'd be more upset if people didn't want my autograph or the press weren't interested in something I'd done.

'The only downside of being in a band is that I feel our life is a step away from reality. I saw this documentary following a group of girls on holiday in Magaluf and it really shocked me – I'd totally forgotten about what normal life is like, when you can do what you want and people don't recognise you.

'All my life, all I've ever wanted is to be famous, to be a star. I still really want that and I'll fight for it – but I want to be happy outside of my job too. I need someone to channel my emotions into. I need someone to make me feel secure.

'I can safely say I've grown up a lot lately. I love the boys, but their play-fighting and jumping on each other can be a bit hard to take sometimes. I know I'm going to sound really boring again, but I'd much rather have an intelligent conversation. I love mucking about sometimes, but not 24/7/52!

WHAT MAKES RITCHIE CRY?

'I'm very emotional and soft – and proud of it. I do get hurt easily, but there's nothing wrong with being sensitive. The last time I cried was because I was working abroad and really missing people. I'm a sucker for sad films. When I went to see *Titanic* with my dad, Sean and J kept saying: "I bet he ends up crying!" And they were right. I bawled my eyes out! Sad, I know, but I don't care!'

'I've learned a lot about people since meeting so many through our work with the band. I'd say I'm becoming good at judging people. I'm not as naive about things as I used to be – I can see through the bullshit a bit better.

'My family love what I'm doing with the band. Mum and Dad were both singers, my Uncle John went to RADA and my auntie, who passed away, was also a singer. My nan, who's in her 80s, pulled me aside at Christmas and said: "I've been so looking forward to seeing you because I always knew that one of my family would make it one day. You've done it for me. I can die happy now."

Wembley at last!

Cool or what?

'There's so much I want for the future. I want the second album to be a great success world-wide and to fly into the charts in America. One day I would love to meet George Michael. I really admire him and think he's got such a great voice. I'd kill for his voice. I also really want to get into films, big time! Acting's always been my lifelong dream. And I want to see more of the world. I know we've been to so many countries with Five but we never stay long enough to really explore or to get to know people. I want to go to Antarctica to see the icebergs, go on safari in Africa, see the Rockies in America and visit the Great Wall of China. I also want to get married and definitely have children. Not much to ask for, huh?!!'

My family mean the world to me and I've always wanted to make them proud. I was so made up by what my nan said, I filled up with tears.

'It's so nice to be able to help my family after all the love and support they've given me over the years. I've bought my brother a car and my mum a Gucci watch to match mine. I do spend a bit on clothes – Harvey Nicks and Selfridges are my fave shops – but then why not?! It's the first time in my life that I've had enough money to go shopping in places like that.

'I am so happy that Five have taken off so well all over the world. But we wouldn't be where we are without the fans. Seeing their faces light up with excitement and pleasure about what we do is the best feeling in the world.'

RITCHIE ON GIRLS

'My ideal girl used to be someone with bright green eyes and blonde hair. But I'm over that now. I used to be really bad, I was always flirting with girls, but that's sooo not me any more. I've grown up more. I want a proper relationship now. There's a certain something that singles a girl out from the others. It's hard to put my finger on it but as soon as I see her I know: "She's the one!" I'm into naughty but nice girls with a bit of oomph! I like it if they've got a bit of the she-devil in them. At the end of the day, I just want a girl who's beautiful on the inside. That quality in a woman is more important to me than what she looks like.'

eUROPE IS home from home for Five. Since the band started out and 'Slam Dunk (da Funk)' soared into the Top 10 (in Italy, Spain, Holland, Germany, Sweden, Denmark, Belgium, Greece and France), the lads have taken more flights to meet their European fans than most people make in a lifetime. It's paid off because today they have millions of loyal supporters across Europe who have fallen head over heels for the band's astonishing talent and charm.

Without doubt, Five are the most successful lad band in Europe, and perform regularly to ecstatic crowds in 100,000-seater stadiums. No top award ceremony is complete without a breathtaking appearance from the lads – who deliver fantastic televised stage performances and never fail to scoop an array of prestigious gongs.

Whenever Five arrive in town there's such a buzz that even the local police sit up and take notice. Let's face it, they don't have any choice. If the police fail to provide a presidential style police cavalcade with motorbike outriders, the thousands of hardcore Five fans bring the city centre to a standstill.

And, like true pop stars, the lads just love it!

MTV Awards

We stayed in Monte Carlo in this really posh, luxury hotel. It was like being in heaven!

SCOTT: I'll never forget the day we were in Germany and got taken out for a day of promotion to a rollerblade and skateboard park. Sean was useless – he could hardly stand up in the skates. He looked like a new-born deer, all over the place – his legs kept shooting out from under him! We couldn't stop laughing – especially when Abs and J started acting like kids. They are really competitive when it comes to dare-devil antics and were almost killing themselves trying to outdo each other's stunts. There was this rollercoaster bit and they were back-flipping all over the place like lunatics. Ritchie just covered his eyes with his hands and kept saying: 'Get an ambulance!'

J: It was madness when we went to Italy. We went to a radio station to do an interview and when we pulled up in the car there were thousands of fans waiting for us. We were only expecting a handful of fans to turn up. But there were so many people in the crowd that the metal railing used to cordon people off had been buckled in half. As soon as we stopped they started rocking the van. It was like we were The Beatles or something!

SEAN: It was such a shock seeing so many fans that it made my head go weird.

RITCHIE: After the radio interview we had to hold on to the security guards and be taken out

It was like
we were
The Beatles
or something!

of the building one at a time. There was too much of a crush so we got dragged back inside. The van was only about seven metres away from the door, so the police made a passageway for us to go through. Sean slowed down a bit and got knocked to the floor and all these girls jumped on top of him. The funniest thing I've ever seen was Rob grabbing him out from underneath this mountain of heaving bodies and bundling him into the van.

J: I was behind Sean and only managed to get half my body in the van. These fans had hold of my bottom half and the lads in the van had hold of my top half. I was crying with laughter. I'd never had such a mad experience in my life. I was off the ground, completely horizontal and thought I was going to get ripped in two. Luckily I kept my trousers on!

SCOTT: We got to play a promo football match too with our Five five-a-side team. Rob used to be a professional footballer so he trains us up and keeps us in shape. We were being followed around by a documentary camera crew and J started really showing off!

J: I did not!

SEAN: Yes he did! He was in goal and tried doing a mega-save, but twisted his ankle really

The biggest choc bar ever

This chocolate needs some breaking

Who's hungry?!!

We love the vibe in Italy and Spain.

Hello Holland!

Yes!!!

J: We had the best night out of the year after we won three TMF Awards in Holland. Sean, Abs, Rob and I went to the after-show party for a bit then went on to this other place called the Beach Club, where the girls walk around in the kind of bikinis that aren't even worth wearing. It was the biggest club I've ever been in. It was so absolutely huge you couldn't see from one end to the other. They cordoned off an area for us to relax in and we drank ridiculous amounts of free drink. I've never seen so many women in bikinis parading around and even the men were wearing shorts. At 6 a.m. we left to go to a boat on the river where they were playing hardcore dance music. We didn't end up getting home until 11 a.m. It was a brilliant night out, so good that I didn't even regret it when I felt totally wrecked the next day.

MTV Studios

ABS: The TMF Music Awards in Holland were amazing. We were nominated for three awards: Best Album, Best International Pop Group and Best Single, along with the likes of Will Smith, Boyzone, Cher and Backstreet Boys in our categories. We didn't think we stood much of a chance, to be honest with you. So you can image how wild we went when we won all three awards! It was amazing. The sort of moment you know you'll remember for the rest of your life.

The Performers

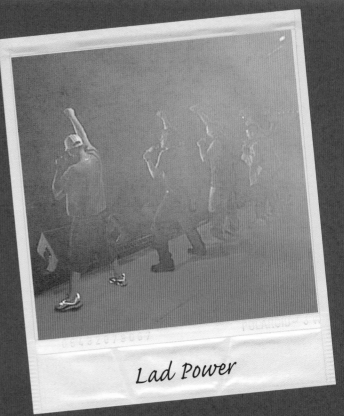

Lad Power

badly. It blew up like a balloon. There was a moment when we thought he wouldn't be able to perform.

ABS: I couldn't believe it when we were invited to perform at the San Remo Music Festival – in front of a 70 million audience. It's a week-long musical event that's mostly Italian artists, but one of the nights they invite foreign guests to appear. This year it was Cher, Mariah Carey and . . . Five! We stayed in Monte Carlo in this really posh, luxury hotel. It was like being in heaven!

RITCHIE: It was all right for you lot. You had a great time, but I was really ill. I was as sick as a dog but – not wanting to let the fans down – I did the show.

ABS: He's a real trooper is our Ritchie!

RITCHIE: You lot got to go out and party all night, but I just managed to get back to the hotel and collapse in my bed.

SEAN: Yeah, the next morning Ritch was a basket-case and we had to get him on a plane and send him home. Mind you, we weren't in a much better state – we'd been out partying so hard we hadn't even got to bed!

ABS: We had some mad nights out in Spain too!

So you can imagine how wild we went when we won all three awards! It was amazing.

Not another award . . .

. . . And another!

SCOTT: Yeah, we've had some brilliant times in Spain. We've done loads of big radio show festivals there. And the fans are as mad as they are in Italy!

J: We've played at the football stadium in Valencia and the arena in Barcelona. There were 8,000 fans and we had to stop the show because so many were fainting and having to be pulled out of the audience.

SEAN: I'd always wanted to go to Monaco and couldn't believe it when Bob and Chris told us that we were going to the San Remo Music Festival to perform alongside Cher and Mariah Carey. I was excited about being on the same bill as major stars, but I was also desperate to go to the famous casino. Me and J went out playing the tables after the concert and it was a good laugh. I felt like I was in a James Bond movie. It's just a shame we didn't win anything!

Mel C and Emma Bunton kept poking us saying: 'You've won – get on up there!'

ABS: Yeah, that was wild. The fans went nuts because we'd stopped the show, so the only way to calm them down was starting again. It was like a mini-riot!

RITCHIE: We love the vibe in Italy and Spain. It's really chilled out.

ABS: Yeah, we always try to go out on the town because there's a really easy vibe and the clubs and music are mad.

J: One of the best things about travelling is getting the chance to go out and explore the local night-life. We were really surprised by Germany. We'd always thought it was a pretty quiet, grey place with no decent night-life.

SEAN: Yeah, but we were so wrong!

J: Me and Sean met a bloke who is really into hip-hop and R'n'B. He took us out on a tour of the night-life. The clubs were wicked. It was wild!

SCOTT: I know I'm a fussy eater, but Germany is one of the hardest places to get food I like.

SEAN, RITCHIE, J and ABS: Oh shut up, Scott!

RITCHIE: You wouldn't believe the lengths we go to when we're abroad to find food for Scott.

RITCHIE: Awards ceremonies are brilliant fun – especially if you win an award that the fans have voted for. The MTV Europe Awards in Milan were cool. George Michael was there and so was Madonna and the Spice Girls. We'd been nominated for the Select UK Award and Bob and Chris knew who'd won but didn't tell us. We thought the likelihood of us winning was zero. When they announced Five as the winners, none of us heard. J was on the phone to his sister and the rest of us were having a chat, so we didn't hear either. Mel C and Emma Bunton were sitting on the table behind us and they kept poking us saying: 'You've won – get on up there!' It was a brilliant surprise.

ABS: Yeah, remember that Christmas when we were in Cologne doing a shoot for *Bliss* magazine? The article was coming out the following March, so to make it look all spring-like we sat on the steps of this famous cathedral having a picnic. Scott wouldn't eat a thing because it wasn't burger, pizza or chips!

The Brits at the MTV Awards in Italy

Abs the alien!

chillin' backstage

What shall I wear?

RITCHIE: I remember that day! All the shopkeepers had their Christmas lights on and they were spoiling the pictures, so our press officer Emma was running round the shops bribing shopkeepers to turn their lights off for a while so we could finish the shoot.

SEAN: Sweden is where the band started out really; where we did the first album. Every time we go there we get that nostalgic feeling. It's like a second home really. I love it.

ABS: Every time I think of Sweden I remember going to the Spy Bar. You had to be over 21 to get in and we were all too young, except for J. I made the big mistake of going to the toilet on my own. These security guards started talking to me in Swedish – having a right go at me they were. I tried to explain that I was with friends but they booted me out of the club. I was waiting outside for three hours until the others came out. They'd been inside having a dance and a drink and thought I was dancing happily by myself somewhere else. I was so fed up!

SEAN: I wish we got more time off when we're away. We've been to France a few times, but we've never stayed long enough to do anything much. Mind you, Ritchie ate some snails once

when we went out to dinner. And we did see the Eiffel Tower – but only from a distance!

SCOTT: Like the time we were in Greece. We got to see the ancient Acropolis – but only from far away. Me and Ritchie went on this mad one pretending we were ancient Romans fighting gladiator battles.

J: The fans were amazing in Greece, weren't they? We were really amazed by the response we got.

RITCHIE: Just like the time when we went back to Denmark after an eight-month gap. It was cool going back there and seeing that we had a million more fans than last time!

ABS: You know, we couldn't get better support than we do from our European fans. They give us the biggest and best highs in the world!

Me and Ritchie went on this mad one pretending we were ancient Romans fighting gladiator battles.

Abs

RICHARD ABIDIN BREEN (better known as Abs) is the coolest, calmest member of Five – laid-back and reflective . . . but very strong-headed! He's quiet and deep and doesn't smoke or drink – but that doesn't stop the 20-year-old from being a serious party animal, renowned for his mad outbursts of outrageous hyperactivity.

Everyone who meets Abs agrees he's a complete sweetheart – a lovely person with a good heart who really cares about people. He's the most easy-going member of Five who rarely gets in a mood and never argues, but he has been known to go into himself and not speak for days.

Abs had an unconventional childhood, growing up in a single-parent family on a tough east-London estate. His dad, Turan, wasn't around when he was a child – although Abs has got to know him better over the past three years. Being an only child, he's very close to his half-Irish mum, Kay, who – given half a chance – does a wicked impersonation of Five, complete with full dance routines!

Abs the DJ

FACT FILE

Name: Abs – Richard Abidin Breen
Date of birth: 29 June 1979
Star sign: Cancer
Height: 5' 9"
Place of birth: Enfield, Essex
Hair colour: Black
Eye colour: Brown with a hint of green
Previous jobs: Helping mum in laundrette
Fave sport: All sport, especially dancing
Hobbies: DJ-ing, music, films, eating out and computer games
Fave food: Mum's shepherd's pie
Distinguishing features: Shaved chest
Family: Mum – Kay; Dad – Turan

Life is sweet and I wouldn't ask for anything to change.

ABS ON LOVE AND ROMANCE

'There's nothing like the feeling of being in love. I don't stop thinking about her – she's the first thing on my mind in the morning and the last thing on my mind at night. I get that glowing feeling inside that tells me she's the girl for me and I just want to be with her all the time. When I'm apart from the one I love, I make up imaginary situations about them in my head and go all soppy. I have to say I am very loyal, very trustworthy and very generous in a relationship but I don't know if I'm romantic. I've been told I am, but I wouldn't like to say so myself – I think I have different ideas about romantic occasions to those of most men! My idea of a perfect romantic day would be to go bungee jumping, then do a tandem sky-dive and then go to Alton Towers and go on all the rides – after a busy day like that we'd need to spend the evening chilling out at home on the sofa with a take-away!'

It was Kay who got her son into performing after taking him to a tap-dancing class. Needless to say Abs – who is one of those people who excels at everything he tries – took to dancing like a duck to water. It came as no surprise when, as soon as he left school, he enrolled in the famous Italia Conti Stage School in London.

Then he joined Five – and, as Abs will tell you, he hasn't looked back since ...

'Life is sweet and I wouldn't ask for anything to change. Before I was in Five I was always either at home or at college. Now I could go to Australia, come home, appear on TV, go to America and sing in front of 10,000 people ... it's amazing!

'So many famous people say they wouldn't recommend fame. But I totally disagree with them. You have to be seriously lucky to be famous – as well as having talent. If you've always wanted to be famous, like I have, and then you achieve your goal, it's brilliant. So the biggest thank you to all you fans out there – without you we would never have done it! I promise you, there's not one bad thing about fame. I'm definitely going to enjoy it for as long as it lasts and make the most of it.

'The past year with Five has been mad. I couldn't believe it when we got the gig with Pepsi. I mean, they've worked with some of the biggest artists in the world. When I was 9 years old I saw this Pepsi ad with Michael Jackson and I thought, "Wow!" To be a part of that is just amazing.

ABS ON GIRLS

'I always like eyes – they're the first thing I notice about a girl. It's all about looks when you first see a girl – but then you get to know their personality and that turns you on as well. I go for a girl if I like the way she presents herself – how she stands and walks. There's always a glow and aura about a person when you see them and like them. I like a girl who doesn't take herself too seriously, is up for a laugh and is honest and genuine. Trust is important too. Without complete trust in a relationship you have nothing.'

'We've done so much and seen so much all around the world – and it's brought us much closer as a band. There was a time when I used to want work to be over so I could go home, but nowadays I'm like: "Isn't there anything extra we can do?!" We're all putting a lot more into Five and it's paying off. I tell you, there is nothing more exciting than performing to our fans or winning awards like MTV's in Europe and TMF's in Holland and having everybody look at you – it makes you feel like a real pop star!

'But even though I love performing, it's also wonderful working with really talented and successful people like our producer Biff. He is so successful and rich, but he's also so normal. I admire people like him, who keep their feet on the ground, more than the really famous people. I'm not naming names, but some stars do let it go to their heads!

'I think I've changed and grown up a lot because of all the experiences I've had with Five. I've become more self-confident and stand up for myself now. Instead of sitting back and letting things wash over me I get more involved. Normally in band meetings I don't say anything, but now I'm more likely to speak up and voice my opinion.

'The downside of being in the band is that I've had a couple of people who I thought were my friends change on me. I don't know what their problem is and I'm too stubborn and pig-headed to find out – but it's upsetting because I've

WHAT MAKES ABS CRY?

'I haven't cried in ages. Even if things go wrong, there isn't any point hanging around in tears – you have to move on. I must admit that sometimes stress makes me cry, when everything gets on top of me or there's problems at home – and I bawled my eyes out through the whole of the film *Titanic*. I might not do it very often, but I'm not afraid of having a good cry because it helps relieve pressure.'

I think I've changed and grown up a lot because of all the experiences I've had with Five.

Jungle cruise

Who's is the biggest?

The train's late . . .

known them all my life. Fortunately my other mates have stayed the same.

'Being in the band has brought me closer to my family in some ways. Me and my grandad have got much closer, for sure. My grandad doesn't like people who fail – he likes winners, so he's dead

I am very loyal, very trustworthy and very generous in a relationship.

proud of Five's success. Being in the band has helped me to help my family. I managed to get my cousins good seats at Wembley for the Cup Final and I can afford to buy them presents. I love buying presents because to me money's just paper and life's about having fun.

'I don't spend that much on myself. I've bought myself some gold-plated mixing decks – I've wanted them for years – and I'm buying bits and bobs for my own recording studio. The only problem is I need to find somewhere to keep them. I'm back living with Mum at the moment because I can't find anywhere to live – and it's doing my head in. I love my mum, but everybody needs somewhere of their own to call home. The trouble is I can't decide whether to buy somewhere in the country or in the middle of London.'

ABS' FUTURE AMBITIONS

'I want Five to be as successful as it possibly can be. My personal ambitions are to be healthy and happy. Eventually – but not yet! – I want to get married and have kids. My mum's dying for me to have a baby so she can be a granny and look after it.'

tHE BUZZ about Five spread across the world fast! With the band scoring several international chart-topping hits and dozens of platinum discs, winning major awards and staging fantastic televised performances to over a billion viewers, it was no wonder that fans in Japan were desperate to witness the Five magic in the flesh.

Even though Five had been on the road for a year – and the lads were delirious with tiredness – they were dying to get to the Land of the Rising Sun to meet their new fans. Amid a hurricane of a promo tour that saw them zig-zagging across the country performing live shows and in-store signings, the lads discovered a culture that was as alien to them as life on another planet!

As Five will tell you, it was like nothing they'd seen before . . .

RITCHIE: Japan was so different to what we expected. I'll never forget the drive into Tokyo from Narita airport. Everything looks pretty normal until you drive over this big bridge – then you suddenly see all these mad modern buildings.

ABS: I think for the first time the whole band were stunned into silence. We were all sitting in the bus with our mouths open.

J: Yeah, it was like something out of the movie *Bladerunner*. Totally futuristic.

SCOTT: We'd expected everywhere to be really traditional and old, so it was a real shock to see all these sci-fi buildings.

J: The modern architecture is amazing – like nothing I've ever seen before. And what makes it seem even more weird is that when you drive out of the city it's like going back a hundred years in time – everything in the country is so old.

It was like something out of the movie *Bladerunner.* Totally futuristic.

SEAN: One of the things I like about going abroad is trying out the local food. I'll usually have a try of anything – however weird it might seem. We were doing a promo show in Tokyo one day and were given some sushi for our lunch. I thought it was going to be those little rice rolls you get wrapped in seaweed, but I opened the box and there was this big dead fish looking at me – eyes and all! And it wasn't even filleted. It freaked me right out. I gave it to a bloke from our record company and he hammered it down like it was fish and chips or something! Just as well it wasn't Scott – he'd probably have fainted if you'd given him something like that to eat!

ABS: The shopping in Japan is amazing. There's an area in Tokyo that's just for electrical equipment – hundreds of massive shops selling the latest technology. Being a serious PlayStation fan I was in seventh heaven! I got so many new games that you can't get anywhere else in the world yet. We were running around like kids in a sweet shop, buying hi-tech Discmans, lap-top computers – you name it we bought it. I was seriously considering buying this amazing wide-screen TV, but then I realized I'd have to lug it around for ages before we got back to London. I even had dreams about that TV – I was so gutted I couldn't buy it!

SEAN: Even though the people in Tokyo look like they have modern, Western lifestyles, when you actually get to meet them you realize just how different culturally they are to us.

J: The one thing I found really fascinating was the etiquette over there. It's so different to anything I've ever seen. Everybody is so polite. They are always bowing to each other and showing their respect.

RITCHIE: Even walking down the street, people are polite. At rush-hour Tokyo is as busy as New York, but the people all walk down the street as if they're in a queue. Nobody rushes or pushes past people, and nobody jay-walks. Even if there's no traffic coming people don't cross the road unless the signs tells them to.

I opened the box and there was this big dead fish looking at me – eyes and all!

RITCHIE: We had a real bonding moment on our last day in Japan. Even though we were as tired as dogs, Abs, Scott and I went out and laid on the floor in the middle of the city at 3 a.m. We were in a circle with our heads touching and we lay there for ages looking up at the sky, the stars and the buildings. We were talking about life – and revealing all our hopes and fears and dreams. It was probably the first time that Abs had really opened up to us. He started telling us about when he was a kid. We lay there for ages – and all these people were walking past looking at us as if we were nuts! It was nearly morning by the time we got back to the hotel. We went back to my room and all passed out together on my bed!

J: The fans are totally different to everywhere else in the world. When we are performing on stage they think it's bad manners to stand up and scream so they just sit there and clap politely.

SEAN: Do you remember our first performance? The fans were so quiet that we thought they hated us! They were so reserved compared to our other fans.

J: All the fans we met were lovely. Every time you speak to girls they cover their mouth with their hand and smile or giggle. We found out that in Japanese society it's considered rude for a girl to smile and show her teeth!

SCOTT: The fans were so well behaved. We did a signing at Virgin and HMV but we never needed security guards because they all lined up in order and waited their turn. There were thousands of girls and there was no carry-on whatsoever. Usually the girls are screaming and have to get dragged away by security.

ABS: Like the fans in the USA – now they are mad! I had one girl flash me – she lifted up her top and showed me everything! I didn't know where to look. You'd never get that in Japan. They're so well behaved.

RITCHIE: The Japanese go wild at night though! I've never seen so many drunk men in business suits in the evening. It's like as soon as they finish working in the office they go and get completely drunk and then stagger home on the train at midnight.

SCOTT: Maybe that's their way of coping with the pressure of life and work.

RITCHIE: Don't go getting any ideas! Five would fall to pieces if we went down that road and drank ourselves silly every time we got stressed!

We were in a circle with our heads touching and we lay there for ages looking up at the sky, the stars and the buildings. We were talking about life – and revealing all our hopes and fears and dreams.

Five bad boys

SCOTT: The presents you get from fans in Japan are amazing. You wouldn't believe the things they gave us – I was totally made up! Nobody has ever given us presents like that. Whenever we did showcases or in-store signings we'd be given things like TVs, radios, Discmans, professional headphones, electrical equipment and even jewellery. It was like ten Christmases all rolled into one! My best memories of Japan are meeting the fans, who were all so sweet and polite.

J: Japan was where I bought my first guitar. We were all out shopping and we saw these amazing electric guitars, and I knew I just had to have one. I'd always wanted one since I was a kid. Scott was the only one who didn't buy one – he said he knew he'd never learn how to play it! Rob, our tour manager, looked at us as if we were mad when we turned up with these big guitar-cases. We've all been trying to learn how to play ever since! I think Ritchie is getting on best. I know he's just written his first song on it – with the only two chords he knows!

Scott

SCOTT ROBINSON is the noisiest member of Five – the fast-talking joker who loves to be the centre of attention. He's hyperactive 24 hours a day.

Even though the other lads say he's the cheekiest in the band, Scott has a sensitive side too. If anybody's got a problem, they know they can go and chat to him because he's a really good listener. He can also talk the hind legs off a donkey, so it's hardly surprising that Scott's addicted to the mobile phone that's always glued to his left ear.

Scott was born to be a star. He went to the famous Sylvia Young Stage School and honed his stagecraft with the likes of Baby Spice Emma Bunton and All Saints sisters Nic and Nat Appleton. He learned confidence on stage and in front of the cameras with appearances on TV programmes like *EastEnders* and *Casualty* and by appearing in the West End stage production of *Peter Pan*.

Scott grew up in Basildon, Essex, with his parents Mick and Sue and his two elder sisters

In Dublin

I think we're this big . . .

FACT FILE

Name: Scott James Tim Robinson

Date of birth: 22 November 1979

Star sign: Scorpio

Height: 5' 11"

Place of birth: Basildon, Essex

Hair colour: Dark brown

Eye colour: Blue

Previous jobs: Acting

Fave sport: Basketball

Hobbies: Skating and music

Fave food: Pizza

Distinguishing features: Long, hairy legs!

Family: Mum – Sue; Dad – Mick; Sisters – Nicola and Hayley

I am very romantic and mushy and never have a problem with showing my feelings.

Nicola and Hayley. Being the youngest in the family and the only boy, he can usually get away with anything. For a start, he's the fussiest eater on the planet – Scott would rather starve himself than eat anything other than McDonald's, pizza or chips, although he's a dab-hand at making flapjack cakes to his own secret recipe.

He's also a real ladies man, who competes with Ritchie for the title of the greatest romantic in Five. With his cheeky charisma and warm personality Scott could charm the knickers off a nun, as he'll tell you himself!

'The past year hasn't been normal, but it's been great! We have worked so hard to make Five a

When I was young I used to say to my parents: 'When I'm famous I'm going to buy you a house.'

3 out of 3!

SCOTT ON LOVE AND ROMANCE

'I know what it's like to be in love – your heart skips a beat, you feel weird and start acting weird too. You can't stop thinking about that person and you phone them all the time, even when you've got nothing to say. I am very romantic and mushy and never have a problem with showing my feelings. I can open up like a burst water-pipe and get all gushy. My perfect romantic moment would be going away on holiday with the girl of my dreams. Sexy couples' holidays are better than a lads' holiday any time. There's nothing more romantic than going somewhere hot and sexy with a hot and sexy girl. I'm a very jealous person in love, to tell you the truth. If I'm in a serious relationship and I can't be with the girl because I'm away, I go mental. I just can't handle the girl going out with her mates when I'm not there. It might sound big-headed but I think I'm a genuinely nice bloke and a good boyfriend. I'm loyal and loving and I'll tell you I love you 10,000 times a day. The trouble with turning into a big pile of mush and acting all nice is that you always end up getting dumped. Girls like it for a bit then they get bored. But I'm not going to change just because girls want a bad lad.'

Pardon?

Check the pose!

success and it's paid off – we're having the best time in the band ever! Last year we were so stressed out, tired and depressed from working so hard that we were falling apart – I was even thinking about having counselling. But now we're really strong. We're five lads sticking together trying to make a dream work.

'I think all the experiences I've had in the band have made me grow up faster. When I joined Five I was 17. Now I'm 20 and I've grown a beard! I can still be really childish – I don't really want to grow up! – but I've got more of a business head on me now and I can be serious. Because I'm dyslexic I can't write, spell or read very well and

WHAT MAKES SCOTT CRY?

'I hate leaving my family and friends when I have to go abroad. When we're away working, I'm all right in the daytime because I've got the other lads in the band around me. But I do get a bit lonely at night and sometimes shed a few tears!'

people think I'm thick. But I'm not. It used to really worry me, but now I'm much more confident about it. I used to be really bothered about what people said about me, but it doesn't matter to me now. I feel strong.

'My family and friends are the most important thing in the world to me and they've been really supportive. If it wasn't for my mates Scott, Leah, Nick, Chris, and the two Dans, Kerry and Kerry, Sarah and Sarah, and everyone up the pub, I don't know how I would have coped (sorry to the people I've missed out – I haven't forgotten you!). Even though I miss home when we're working abroad, knowing that my mates will be

SCOTT ON GIRLS

'I like girls with lovely eyes and lips. What really makes a girl stand out to me is if she's girlish because I like sweet-looking girls. It's really important to me that a girl is natural and down to earth. I definitely don't like flashy, pushy girls.'

SCOTT'S FUTURE AMBITIONS

'I want Five to carry on and conquer the world! All I want is to feel stable, secure and have somebody to love who loves me. If I had one wish in the world it would be that my nan got better – she's got Alzheimer's disease. I love her so much, but I haven't visited her for four years because I couldn't cope with seeing her ill. I wanted to remember my nan when she was well, doing high-kicks in the living room. But I've decided to go and see her now because I don't want to lose her without seeing her again. My grandad has nursed and cared for my nan so brilliantly. That's what real love is all about – loving each other and staying loyal even when things get hard.'

there for me when I get back keeps me going.

'I do get terribly homesick: I'm just a normal lad from Essex living my dream. But I love being on stage performing – it's the best feeling in the world. There isn't a buzz like seeing an audience getting into the songs. And it's wild going to a country you've never visited before and meeting thousands of new fans.

'Just a couple of years ago I was broke, so it's really nice having made some money. I've bought myself a lap-top computer and a video camera and some furniture for my new house. It's lovely to be able to help your family. I've bought my

dad a Previa van with blacked-out windows and I got him a job, driving me around. My sister Hayley is having a baby in September and I reckon it's going to be a boy. I just can't wait to be an uncle – think of all the toys I can buy!

'When I was young I used to say to my parents: "When I'm famous I'm going to buy you a house!" And I've kept to my end of the bargain – I've bought them a big, big house. They keep saying: "It's big enough for you to move in, Scott," but I'm happy where I am. It's really nice having my own place. It's good to go back there and chill out. I can walk around naked and not bother anybody!

Me and Dad

UK & Ireland

SEAN, SCOTT, J, Ritchie and Abs will never forget that the UK is where it all started for Five. From the moment the band won the Smash Hits Best New Tour Act award and watched 'Slam Dunk (da Funk)' crash into the charts at Number 10, they knew they were on the road to stardom.

The lads say that Five's success has only been possible because of the amazing support they've received from their UK fans – fans who've helped them rack up 5 scorching Top 10 singles, a Number 1 debut album and a cluster of prestigious awards!

Five have graced the cover of over 30 top magazines and been on more photo shoots than most models could ever begin to imagine. They've also linked up with confectionery giants Cadbury's and MTV Europe for a massive promotion campaign.

What more could Five possibly want? Well, the lads will tell you that the one thing they're dying for is the release of their second album and the UK tour – which kicks off at the start of the new millennium!

Five can't wait for the year 2000. As they say... 'There's no place like home!'

SEAN: One of the best things we've done in England was the Smash Hits Awards. Last year we got Best Newcomer and this time we headlined the show and won awards! The reception from the fans was fantastic. We would never have gone from support to headline act if we hadn't had such brilliant support from our home fans.

SCOTT: Yeah, Smash Hits was great. We won a lot of awards!

RITCHIE: Best Band and Best Haircut for Scott's barnet!

J: The Brits was great fun too! We didn't mind that we didn't win the award for Best British Newcomer – we were just amazed and proud to be nominated.

SCOTT: I'm such a home bod that I love it when we work in England. We've had some right

Sound Republic

The best thing about England is coming back.

Everybody get up!

SCOTT: I'll never forget the day I got the chance to play basketball with the London Leopards. I was made up! I've been a basketball fan since I was a kid. I used to play at school and I was quite good – if I may say so myself! (I'm not a big-head, honest!) I got a right shock when I arrived at the training ground because all the blokes towered over me like giants – they must have been over 7 feet tall! I did a basic skills training session with the team and then we played a game. It was fantastic – I even scored a few times! Then I taught the team the dance that goes with the chorus of 'When The Lights Go Out'. It was a right laugh – lots of fans had come down to see the action and they sung for us while we danced! It was tops when the trainer said that if I ever wanted to leave Five he'd give me a job in his team as a point guard!

Abs, J & Sean in action!

When we're all together we get very competitive.

laughs shooting our videos. Filming 'Everybody Get Up' was mad – we were throwing paint and chairs around – and being allowed to do it! But I did feel for the dancers – they spent the whole time being covered in paint and then washed off with ice-cold water sprinklers. If you notice, we didn't get wet or messy once in the video, and behind us there are all these poor wet and bedraggled people. I felt so guilty about it I even considered getting wet too!

SEAN: We are very lucky, you know, in every respect. We did this big tie-up with Cadbury's and MTV Europe – and we got lots of free chocolate.

SCOTT: What with Cadbury's and Pepsi, we're sorted. All we need now is to do something with McDonald's!

ABS: I think we have the luckiest job in the world. Who else gets the chance to go to places like Chessington Zoo and have a laugh mucking about on all the rides – and call it work?!

J: Like the time we went rollerblading under the Westway in London. Sean was hopeless – he just couldn't get the hang of it. Abs, who had never rollerbladed before in his life, was brilliant – he was doing back-flips and going up ramps.

What with Cadbury's and Pepsi, we're sorted. All we need now is to do something with McDonald's!

Did we win then?

When we're all together we get very competitive. I seem to remember that Scott got the hump!

RITCHIE: The shoot we did for *Live and Kicking!* magazine was excellent. We stayed at the Hilton Hotel in Park Lane in the Presidential Suite! I can say that I've used the same loo as a president! It was the most amazing suite. We had three bedrooms, two living rooms, three balconies and bathrooms all over the place. The views were amazing – we could even see the gardens of Buckingham Palace. We did shots all round the suite – Scott on the balcony, Abs on the phone and Sean in the bed. And guess what? Sean fell asleep!

SCOTT: That's right. Rob spent ages trying to wake him up!

J: Rob has a lot of physical and verbal abuse to put up with, looking after us. Not long ago we were at South West Studios, doing a photo shoot. Rob was sitting in a chair and we tied him up with cling-film. He went along with it, thinking we were playing around. Two hours later, after Ritchie squidged a Mars Bar in his mouth, Sean smacked him on the head with a tablespoon and we all poured water over him and stabbed his feet with forks, we let him go – but only because his hands had gone blue!

RITCHIE: I am a lifelong Aston Villa supporter, so it didn't take much persuading to get me to turn up in my kit for a tour around the ground and a training session! It was fascinating visiting the changing rooms and seeing where the players prepare for a match – and walking out through the tunnel like you see on TV. When I got out on the pitch and touched the hallowed turf it was a dream come true. It was all I could do to stop myself from digging out a little bit of the turf to keep as a souvenir! There was a lot more to the training than I thought. We're all pretty fit in the band but it was exhausting! I practised my headers into goal for about an hour and it nearly killed me! Mind you, I can't think of a better way to die!

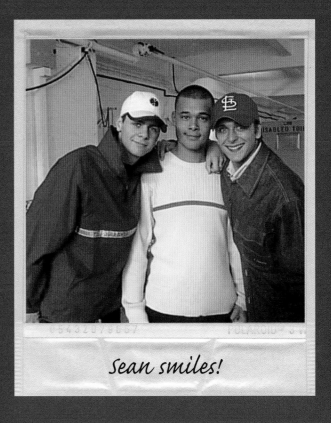

Sean smiles!

I'm a speed freak. I just love that adrenaline rush you get when you go fast or do dangerous things.

ABS: I'm a speed freak. I just love that adrenaline rush you get when you go fast or do dangerous things. When I was offered the chance to drive a Formula First car at Brands Hatch – and go 0-60 mph in under six seconds – I was there like a flash. We had a serious briefing session where they taught us how to race safely and then we were let out on a trial run in a BMW First car. I had an instructor go around the track with me a few times just to make sure I wasn't a hazard on the road – he said I took the corners a bit too fast! – and then I was let loose in a single-seater Formula First. It was wicked racing round the track. I nearly had an accident when I saw a little squirrel on the tarmac. I didn't have the heart to run it over so I swerved to miss it and nearly came off the track! I have to say that racing around Brands was the most thrilling thing I've ever done. I loved it!

J: I suppose I'm the one out of the band who does the most silly things. I've done some mad and dangerous stuff in my life, but the one thing I've always wanted to do is a parachute jump. It was brilliant when I got the chance to jump. I was a bit nervous when I arrived, but then I was given a briefing and the next thing I knew I was in a plane with a parachute on my back! It took us 35 minutes going through the clouds watching everything on the ground getting smaller and smaller until we got up to 11,000 feet. I was attached to my instructor's harness and suddenly we just jumped out. I was a bit scared but I didn't have time to have second thoughts. We accelerated through the air at 240 mph in eight seconds – faster that a Formula 1 car! The speed, fear and adrenaline as I was free-falling through the sky gave me the most amazing buzz I've ever had. It was superb!

The speed, fear and adrenaline as I was free-falling through the sky gave me the most amazing buzz I've ever had.

Who's talking?

Who's singing?

SEAN: I've been into Rugby League since I was a kid. Dad and me always went to watch games back home in Leeds. I used to play for the school and trained three times a week and played every Sunday. But I stopped when I got into Five. I was made up when the London Broncos offered to let me train with them for a day! They had me running about all over the place, making passes, trying to get past defenders and even kicking goals. Most of the blokes were twice my size, but they were really sound and friendly. I was worn out by the end of the day – knackered actually – but it was definitely worth it!

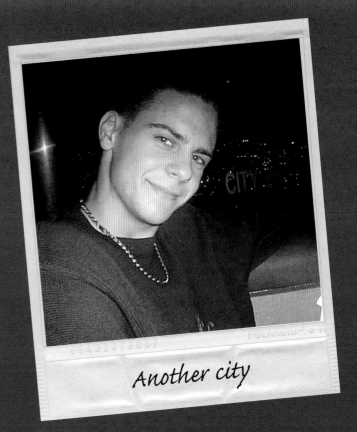

Another city

SCOTT: Yeah, and when J tried to cut the masking tape off his wrists he cut Rob's jumper to pieces. Rob was so angry!

RITCHIE: He's going to get us all back for that one day, you know. He said he'd do it one lad at a time!

ABS: We were just larking around. Normally we're quite okay, but we have been known to tip beds up and wreck each other's rooms.

SCOTT: I seem to remember that happening to me when we were in Dublin. I never found out who did it!

RITCHIE, SEAN, J and ABS: It wasn't me!

SEAN: We love going to Dublin – it's a really friendly place. We've spent a lot of time out there recording our second album. It's very chilled. You can go out to a pub, get recognised and after about 15 minutes people don't really bother you any more.

J: It isn't really like work when we record with our producer Biff out there. It's more like a holiday – really chilled and laid-back.

ABS: Do you remember that time when we were being followed around by loads of fans in the street? Rob was worried and wanted to get us inside somewhere, out the way. He had a word with a landlord in a pub who took us through the back entrance. He was a brilliant bloke. He gave us free drinks all evening and even took us out to a club!

Another waiting room

SCOTT: I have to say that the best thing about England is coming back. It's always good arriving at Heathrow airport and seeing our British fans. Then we know we're home!

Five
on
Five

aBS, SEAN, J, Ritchie and Scott have wanted to be superstars all their lives – and they've spent the past two years working 24/7 to make the dream come true. As the hard rockin' popsters will tell you, the road to fame hasn't been easy. However, the hard work has paid off and their talent has shone through – today Five are international pop stars!

But what happens, behind the scenes, when five lads from five different backgrounds spend most of their working life joined at the hip? Do they become friends or rivals? One thing's for sure, Five have been on the road for a long time – and they've got to know each other almost better than they know themselves.

So let's listen up to what the lads have got to say as they spill the beans on what Five are really like ...

Scott

J on SCOTT: There isn't a malicious bone in Scott's body. He wouldn't purposefully harm anybody – in fact he'd go out of his way not to. Even if you've made a nasty remark he doesn't retaliate. He's a really nice lad, actually, but I do think Scott could get a lot more out of what we're doing. I think we all agree that Scott just sleeps far too much! When we were in DisneyWorld and had a few hours off to go round the park, Scott went back to his hotel and phoned his family. I know for a fact that, if he's not careful, when the band finishes he'll look back and regret all the opportunities he's passed up on.

There isn't a malicious bone in Scott's body.

SEAN on SCOTT: Scott has the worst taste in clothes. He just puts things on without even thinking about whether they go together or not. Sometimes he looks right odd. But he's a top geezer. He's a real loyal friend who'd never let you down.

ABS on SCOTT: Scott is always friendly. You can be pissed off with him and he won't have it – he doesn't like arguing. He'll try and make friends. Scott is very charming. He can put it on whenever you need it!

RITCHIE on SCOTT: He's always hyperactive and a right joker. But even though he's a nutter, he's got a really sensitive side too. He's a really good listener. If I've got a problem I know I can go and have a serious chat with him. He really cares about other people.

RITCHIE on ABS: Abs isn't very good at showing his feelings. He shuts himself off. If he's in a bad mood he won't talk. He just puts his hand up like he's saying: 'Get out of my face.' Abs is wonderful at listening to other people's problems and helping them, but he should let other people help him.

SCOTT on ABS: Abs changes his sideburns every day, without fail. And he never gets a joke ever! You tell him a joke, wait for the reaction and after a long pause he says: 'I don't get it.' But he's the easiest-going in the band, he's got his head screwed on and he really knows where he's going.

SEAN on ABS: He's a very kind, generous person – he'd give anything away if you asked him for it. He's just like his mother. Sometimes he goes into himself and gets really quiet, but he doesn't do that so much any more. But I'm quiet myself and I wouldn't say it was a bad thing anyway.

Abs getting down

J on ABS: When we first started in the band Abs used to run a bit hot and cold. You'd be getting on and then he'd go all frosty and wouldn't speak properly to you for a couple of days. But recently we've become really good friends. If he's your friend he'd do anything for you. He's probably the most thoughtful, generous person on the planet.

He's a very kind, generous person.

Abs

J on RITCHIE: I love Ritchie to bits. It's like all the band – there isn't anything I wouldn't sacrifice for them. Ritchie is so warm and giving but he's one of the most naive people on the planet. People see it as an endearing quality, but sometimes it isn't. I'd hate to think that people might take advantage of his kind nature.

SEAN on RITCHIE: With no disrespect to Ritchie, he can have his moments when his hair doesn't go right. We call it 'A Ritchie Moment'. The rest of the time he's a really nice bloke. Ritchie spends the most amount of money on silly things, usually clothes. He bought these funny shoes that looked like slippers – and he went out in them! Ritchie is just a hippy. If we argue he says: 'Stop killing the vibe – be friends.'

ABS on RITCHIE: Ritchie's on my hippy level. We sat on a plane once going to America talking for the whole journey about the universe and what happens in space. We came up with these mad conclusions about the world. He's definitely the most sensitive in the band – he likes a good cry. I think everybody agrees, we rely on him to be charming – he's very good at pretending not to be tired when he's knackered.

SCOTT on RITCHIE: Ritchie's a genuinely nice bloke. He's always got time for you. But if he's in a bad mood he'll jump down your throat. I hate his tone of voice when he's shouting. I always say: "Change your tone!" And he's always flicking his hair, which really annoys me. I think the girls find Ritchie the most charming in the band. They wouldn't be wrong either because he is the most charming, kind, warm bloke you'll ever meet.

Nice specs!

I think girls find Ritchie the most charming in the band.

Ritchie

Sean

SCOTT on SEAN: Sean is definitely the most laid-back person ever – even if he won the Lottery he wouldn't show how excited he was! It's funny when Sean gets annoyed – he never shouts or gets angry, he gets his own back in a more subtle way. He'll walk past and call you names under his breath or he'll gently head-butt you or flick your ear or slap you round the head. Sean could do well with girls, but he doesn't bother. He never goes over and talks to them. On the rare occasions that he does, he'll go and say something crap like 'Do you come here often?' and spoil it straight away!

J on SEAN: We share a lot of interests and I think we're very similar. I got on with Sean from the start – he's like my younger brother. He could do a lot more for himself though. If Sean could do something to enhance his life that takes a bit of effort he just doesn't bother. He can be so lazy – it drives me mad!

RITCHIE on SEAN: Everyone thinks Sean's shy, but he's not at all. He's got a very dry sense of humour. But he does really niggly, irritating things to bug you when he's in a mood. You can talk to Sean because he's quite old-headed – even though he's only 18. He's very mature and sensible with his money.

ABS on SEAN: Sean is so laid-back and chilled. But he's got this thing he does that really winds me up. It's called Dapper The Rapper – he rolls his jeans into his socks and starts talking in this weird accent. If you're tired it batters your head. Apart from his occasional weird one, he's always tired or sleeping. He's so laid-back that half the time he doesn't buy anything when we're out shopping because he literally can't be bothered to take his bank card out of his pocket and use it. I swear Sean must be the wealthiest member of the band. He doesn't feel the need to spend any money – ever. He's only bought a

camera since he's been in the band. I can see it. One day we'll all be asking Sean to lend us a tenner!

He's got a very dry sense of humour.

SCOTT on J: He will scream and shout and call you all the names under the sun. But J will always apologise to you afterwards. He has a quick temper but he's a really honourable bloke. J could be really successful with the girls, but he doesn't bother. If a girl's looking at him and it's blatantly obvious she really fancies him he won't go over and talk to her.

SEAN on J: At the beginning of the group I could relate to J better than the others because he was more like the kind of person I was used to. Growing up in Leeds I'd never had the experience of meeting a different sort of person to me, like Ritchie or Abs or Scott. I had to adapt and J helped me. But he can be very loud. When you're tired, it's the last thing you need.

ABS on J: J's got a lot of experience because he's the oldest. In a funny way you feel like you don't have to worry because you know he's there, making sure everything's okay. But J spends a lot of time in front of the mirror sorting out his hair and beard. Sometimes he's at it for more than an hour!

RITCHIE on J: He's a weird cookie sometimes. He flips out, but you can really talk to him. If he's in a good mood he's a brilliant bloke, but if he's in a bad mood he shouts. He wastes a lot of energy shouting rather than listening.

How did we get here?

He has a quick temper but he's a really honourable bloke.